FINDING a CAREER

Careers If You Like Writing

Robert Green

San Diego, CA

About the Author

Robert Green started his writing career thinking up jacket copy and picture captions for books on topics ranging from Vikings to Victorian explorers. He later earned a master's degree in journalism from New York University and another in East Asian Studies from Harvard University. He now works as a journalist covering the politics of Hong Kong and Taiwan for the Economist Intelligence Unit and for Oxford Analytica and regularly reviews books on East Asian subjects. He has also written more than forty nonfiction books for young adults.

Picture Credits

Cover: Shutterstock.com/neneus
11: Depositphotos
34: Depositphotos
71: Depositphotos

© 2017 ReferencePoint Press, Inc.
Printed in the United States

For more information, contact:

ReferencePoint Press, Inc.
PO Box 27779
San Diego, CA 92198
www.ReferencePointPress.com

LIBRARY OF CONGRESS CATALOGING-IN-PUBLICATION DATA

Names: Green, Robert, 1969- author.
Title: Careers if you like writing / by Robert Green.
Description: San Diego : ReferencePoint Press, Inc., [2017] | Series: Finding a career | Includes bibliographical references and index.
Identifiers: LCCN 2016011796 (print) | LCCN 2016024363 (ebook) | ISBN 9781682820100 (hardback) | ISBN 9781682820117 (eBook)
Subjects: LCSH: Authorship--Vocational guidance--Juvenile literature. | Writing services--Vocational guidance--Juvenile literature.
Classification: LCC PN159 .G74 2017 (print) | LCC PN159 (ebook) | DDC 808.02--dc23
LC record available at https://lccn.loc.gov/2016011796

CONTENTS

Introduction: Putting Your Writing to Work

Much of the writing that students do is either creative writing—poetry, personal essays, and short stories—or academic writing backed up by academic research. For students who find themselves captivated by the written word and by the complexity of language with all its rules and exceptions, the workplace at first glance might seem like an alien environment. So much of that academic and creative writing that punctuates school semesters is just not the kind of thing that employers are looking for when hiring new employees.

Yet it turns out that the written word has become more important than ever in the workplace—though perhaps in forms different from the writing traditionally emphasized in a classroom. A survey of 120 major American companies by the National Committee on Writing for America's Families, Schools, and Colleges found that two-thirds of salaried employees have some writing responsibilities and that half of all the companies take writing skills into account when hiring new employees. "The inability to write clearly and effectively communicate through the written word significantly impacts your ability to land a new job or promotion," explains Stephanie Heald-Fisher in "Having Good Writing Skills Is Important for the Business World," an article on a Globe University and Minnesota School of Business blog.

Writing, Writing Everywhere

In fact, it turns out that people are writing more than ever before in their daily lives, even when they don't think of themselves as writers or literary types. A quick survey of a coffee shop twenty years ago might have turned up a few people writing. Perhaps one was working on the next great American novel; perhaps another was writing a longhand letter to her boyfriend to call the whole thing off. But most of the coffee shop loungers would have been reading newspapers or chatting with friends.

Today coffee shops are brimming with people intently pecking away at laptops. So just what are all those people typing? The answer is just about everything. You might still find someone who is working on the next great American novel. But you are more likely to find people e-mailing, posting news stories and comments on social media, and blogging about their interests. Much of today's writing is the result of momentous technological changes—in a word, the ability to use laptops and mobile phones to keep in touch from anywhere. Those devices, as much as they have killed the social environment of a coffee shop, have led to a constant stream of communication that is highly relevant to the workplace.

In fact, many of the forms of writing going on at coffee shops can be the seeds of a career putting words to work. When friends explain in e-mails and on social media sites how their new iPhones work or how a new app makes it easier to do something that was difficult before, they are on the road to technical writing. When social media users curate news stories on their personalized social media pages by posting and sharing, they are performing a basic function of an editor—sorting content for their audience. And when online enthusiasts share a new recipe or describe a trip abroad, they are engaging two flourishing forms of blogging— food and travel writing.

Even the posting of opinions and comments on social media sites represents the exercise of a highly marketable skill—the ability to convince others through well-reasoned written arguments, humor, or evidence. The writers of advertising copy try to catch our interest by forming clever narratives that excite our imagination and our interest in a product. Grant writers employ argument to secure funding to save local rivers, explore social issues, or raise money for educational programs. And lawyers spend much of their time drafting briefs, arguments, appeals, and other written documents to convince a judge that their argument should prevail in a legal dispute. The ability to convince through the written word extends through many diverse professions—from screenwriters, who convince us that a story is worth watching, to speechwriters, who convince us that the speaker can make a point effectively and memorably. Words are used to sell products, explain ideas and positions, entertain, and convince someone that one position should win out over another.

Writing as an Indispensable Job Skill

None of this is being lost on employers. In a survey conducted by the Graduate Management Admission Council, the organization that administers the standardized test for business schools, 86 percent of corporate recruiters said strong communication skills were a priority. An NBC online news article, "Why Johnny Can't Write, and Why Employers Are Mad," quotes William Ellet, a writing professor, explaining how essential writing is to future employment. "Recruiters and companies are saying, 'Send us a writing sample, and if you don't meet our standards for communication, we are not hiring you,'" he points out.

In fact, people in offices today increasingly look like a mirror image of people in coffee shops. Workers communicate by e-mail and instant messaging. Employers use blog posts to drum up interest in new products and services. They tweet about their successes and blog about their future plans. Social media, and communicating over the Internet in all forms, is now a major part of workplace communications. "Writing skills are still important. In fact, it can be argued that they are even more important now than ever," writes Sarah Wright on Study.com, an academic website. "It's always been important for professionals and academics to use proper grammar and communicate well, but now, it's increasingly important for more people to have good writing skills."

Writing, therefore, is best thought of not as a career choice in itself but as an indispensable skill that facilitates entry into many professions. And so, if you like to write and you can produce well-crafted prose, there will be no shortage of employers eager to put those skills to work—no matter what profession you choose.

Journalist

A Few Facts

Pay
The median annual income for reporters, correspondents, and broadcast news analysts was $37,200 in 2014.

Getting the News
Fifty-six percent of US adults report using a cell phone to get news; 29 percent report using a tablet.

Top News Source
The most popular source for online news in 2015 was the Yahoo!-ABC News website.

Shrinking Newspaper Jobs
Jobs for full-time journalists at US newspapers fell from 36,700 in 2013 to 32,900 in 2015.

Future Job Outlook
A projected decline of 9 percent through 2022, but new online media may bring new growth.

What Does a Journalist Do?

A quick scan of articles about journalism indicates a profession undergoing revolutionary change. "Forget Brian Williams: Journalism Is Changing from the Bottom Up," trumpets a *Forbes* magazine article about how traditional television newscasters like Brian Williams are being replaced by digital media, social media posts, and citizen journalism written by everyday people around the country.

People today get their news from a variety of sources. While newspapers have declined over the years, online news has grown dramatically. There were 1,878 American newspapers in 1940, but that number had declined to 1,331 by the end of 2014, according to Bloomberg News. Among traditional media sources, sometimes called "legacy" media, television remains the most common source of news, while the once mighty newspaper has seen its readership shrink. So where are people getting their news today? The answer is that people are increasingly reading the news on their cell phones, laptops, and tablets. Journalists have followed this industry trend with their feet, picking up and moving to new online news organizations such as ProPublica, the *Huffington Post*, and Vice.

But all that excitement and change over the platforms for the delivery of news can be deceptive. Journalists, in fact, rely on the same job skills today that they did in the past, whether they publish stories in newspapers or on websites. Their primary job, unchanged for generations, is to deliver new information in a professional manner.

The Making of a News Story

So just what goes into the making of a news story? First, a journalist gathers information on a new development—a local fire or the new law passed by Congress, for example. The journalist does this by seeking out facts, both through interviewing people involved in the story and by gathering information from public records and other documents. By doing research and interviewing people involved in a story, the journalist seeks to answer the most important basics of all stories—who, what, when, where, why, and often how a story came to be. Once those questions are

Finding the Story

"I like digging out information that hasn't been reported and then presenting it in a way that readers will understand and value. It's great when you see someone reading and enjoying a piece you've written. Journalism allows you to meet and talk to a huge range of interesting people and is immensely varied. In one week I might be working on an interview with a singer, a piece about coffee shops paying tax and an investigation into an unsolved murder. I think I'd get bored just working on one thing all the time."

Susannah Butter, "A Day in the Life of . . . an *Evening Standard* Journalist," Reading Agency, 2013. http://readingagency.org.uk.

answered, the reporter writes up the story in a way that conveys information in a quickly understandable manner.

Between writing and publication, a number of steps are required to ensure the quality of a news story. Once complete, the story is submitted to an editor, who checks for quality and points out any weaknesses in the story. Once approved, the written article is then proofread by a copy editor, who checks for mistakes in grammar and spelling and perhaps adds a headline to the story. Each of those functions is performed by a professional also considered a journalist. Each is a job opportunity for people who like to write but perform different functions in the process of producing journalism.

College Degree Required

A college degree is required for most journalism jobs. Some journalists have degrees in journalism, which involves the academic study of the industry and the daily practice of the craft of writing, editing, and broadcasting stories. But it is not necessary to study journalism to be a journalist. A journalist who writes about business, for example, might have a bachelor's degree in economics. A science writer might have concentrated in the sciences in college, thus obtaining an understanding of the field, known as a "beat" in journalism lingo, that he or she focuses on as a journalist. The most important thing to remember is that if you can find good stories and write them well, most employers will consider you for employment no matter what subject you studied in college.

Breaking In to the Business

Because journalism is a craft, it requires practice. The good news is that there are endless opportunities to practice journalism. It is rare for a high school or college not to have a newspaper, and increasingly schools regularly produce radio and TV broadcasts. Since schools are always looking for new content, it is easy to get an assignment if you can find a story worth covering. This is essentially free job training. All you need are good ideas and the willingness to give up some of your free time to practice the demanding craft of journalism.

Many city neighborhoods and suburban towns also have local newspapers or news websites. They may or may not pay for your stories, but they will certainly demand that you produce good copy (the basic text of a news story). They will give you a chance to publish your stories and build a portfolio of clips—a collection of your work that can be presented to potential employers.

By pitching (proposing) stories to different publications and writing them up for publication, you are already working as a professional journalist, even if you are not doing it full-time for a news organization or magazine. This is the life of the freelancer, an old term for a mercenary, or one who offers his sword (lance, in this case) to those who can pay (hopefully). Freelancing is a tough way to make a living, but it is an excellent way to build up your résumé and learn the skills demanded by employers.

Media outlets also train journalists by allowing them to work part-time or on a short-term basis through internships. These might be paid, but often they are not. Internships can be quite competitive. Landing an internship or a journalism job takes tenacity and the willingness to work hard. "When I set my eyes on a particular gig I'd love to land," writes Alexandra Posadzki, a young reporter from Canada on the *So, You Want to Be a Journalist?* blog, "I often spend months in advance pitching and writing stories to make sure I have the kind of clippings that the employer would most value."

Skills and Personality

Journalism unquestionably requires persistence and curiosity. No story can be written without both characteristics. But just what type of personality best fits the profession? Some journalists pound the pavement, doing interviews and gathering facts. This suggests that an outgoing person is more likely to find satisfaction as a journalist. But then comes the writing of the story, the editing, and the proofreading. These functions are largely solitary

10

A television news reporter does an interview and a cameraman films it for later broadcast. Television is still the most common source of news, but online news organizations are gaining audiences and clout.

and require the ability to concentrate intensely with little interaction. This suggests that introverts might also find job satisfaction working as a journalist. In short, almost any personality type can fit into this multifaceted profession.

A more overarching characteristic is the ability to think logically, to figure out what makes a good story and what information is needed to tell that story. It takes a commitment to ferreting out the truth of things, while also being highly skeptical of what people are saying. "As a journalist, you are always seeking the truth," Michael Konopasek, a reporter for KWTV in Oklahoma City, wrote on the *Work in Entertainment* blog in December 2015. "Sometimes it is a challenge to find, since interviewees won't always be honest with you, so as a news reporter it's important to be skeptical. As you become more experienced in your field, you will find that these challenges are easier to tackle."

Who's Hiring?

With the decline of print media, the job market has become more competitive. Young journalists will more likely seek out jobs in television or at newer online media outlets. A search of the job-hunting website Indeed in early 2016 revealed 1,723 job openings in journalism, with 141 jobs listed recently. The employers ranged from trade publications to television to online publications. Vice, a rapidly growing online news site and TV producer, listed forty-three job openings in February 2016, and it is rapidly expanding its overseas bureaus. Thirty of the largest digital-only news organizations account for about three thousand jobs, according to the *State of the News Media 2014* report from the Pew Research Center. The journalism jobs of the future will be found mostly online.

Working Conditions

Journalism provides a wide variety of work environments—from offices to war zones. Reporters are often out chasing stories and conducting interviews. Editors are generally bound to a desk in the offices of the publication or broadcaster.

An all-important feature of a journalist's work life is the deadline. For newspapers and broadcasters, this quite often arrives once a day; for magazines it might be weekly or monthly. Online news publishers, in theory, have the freedom to publish whenever their stories are ready, not having to wait for a printer to publish a hard copy. But competition from TV and other online news sources creates pressure to publish as often as possible. Thus, instead of having one deadline a day, an online publisher will be scrambling to beat the competition by publishing stories as quickly as humanly possible. In general, therefore, journalism is a demanding profession. How stressful or rewarding that is will largely stem from how much you relish the challenge.

Money

As a profession, journalism is not high paying, though there are exceptions. TV newscasters, for example, are celebrities in their own right and earn salaries more commonly found in the higher reaches of the entertainment industry. Diane Sawyer was paid about $12 million in 2015 for her work as an ABC News anchor. But most journalists will never make that kind of money. And in fact, most do it for the love of the profession, which is a good thing since the median annual income for reporters, correspondents, and broadcast news analysts was $37,200 in May 2014, according to the US Department of Labor's Bureau of Labor Statistics.

Climbing the Job Ladder

Opportunities for advancement in journalism are plentiful, but there are some pitfalls. A cub reporter, or a journalist just starting out in the business, can build a career by excelling at the craft and obtaining more prestigious assignments. The range of employers also makes it easy to change employers to find better job prospects, leveraging experience at one news outlet into a better job at another.

Yet for those who like to write, advancement can lead to less writing. Editors, who write less than reporters, are generally paid better. And the highest-paid journalists often spend more time managing and directing publications than crafting stories. If writing is what you enjoy most, you will probably be happiest avoiding the highest rungs of the journalism ladder, unless you desire the dizzying salary of a famous TV newscaster.

What Is the Future Outlook for Journalists?

Journalism is undergoing a thorough shake-up as a profession. As newspapers have declined, Internet sources have stepped in to fill the breach, but no one knows exactly where this trend will lead. The US Department of Labor predicts that the number of journalism jobs will decline by 9 percent from 2014 to 2024. But this is by no means a certainty, because no one knows just how many new jobs will be created online.

Find Out More

American Society of News Editors
209 Reynolds Journalism Institute
Missouri School of Journalism
Columbia, MO 65211
phone: (573) 884-2405
website: http://asne.org

The American Society of News Editors helps cultivate high ethical and professional standards for professional journalists. It holds annual conferences for news editors, promotes dialogue on the industry, and provides information for journalists on its website.

Association of Magazine Media
757 Third Ave., 11th Floor
New York, NY 10017
phone: (212) 872-3700
website: www.magazine.org

The Association of Magazine Media is a nonprofit organization that represents 175 media publishers. It works with government and industry to help expand the magazine industry and holds conferences to explore new ideas in magazine publishing.

National Association of Broadcasters

1771 N St. NW
Washington, DC 20036
website: www.nab.org

The National Association of Broadcasters represents the interests of radio and TV broadcasters. It is both a lobby group and an advocacy group promoting the interests of the industry. Its website includes industry news, jobs links, and important news on the regulation of the airwaves. It also seeks to educate broadcasters through seminars and other educational services.

Newspaper Association of America

4401 Wilson Blvd., Suite 900
Arlington, VA 22203
phone: (571) 366-1000
website: www.naa.org

The Newspaper Association of America is a central clearinghouse for information on the newspaper industry. Its website features news on the newspaper industry and statistics on readership, circulation, revenue, and other topics essential to the business of newspaper journalism. It also features links to job openings and provides information on trends in the job market.

Society of Professional Journalists

Eugene S. Pulliam National Journalism Center
3909 N. Meridian St.
Indianapolis, IN 46208
phone: (317) 927-8000
website: www.spj.org

The Society of Professional Journalists works to ensure legal protections for journalists guaranteed under the First Amendment of the US Constitution and to improve the ethical standards of working journalists. It has chapters across the United States, and its website provides information on legal issues pertaining to the media, ethical codes of conduct, and a host of other information.

Blogger

A Few Facts

Popularity

About 6.7 million people blog on blogging sites, and 12 million people blog via social networks.

Number of Blogs

There are more than 1.52 billion blogs on the Internet.

Marketing

Nearly 40 percent of US companies use blogs for marketing purposes.

Boosting Sales

Companies that blog receive 97 percent more links to their website.

Corporate Blogging

Thirty-four percent of Fortune 500 companies now maintain active blogs.

What Does a Blogger Do?

The word *blog* is the shortened form of *weblog*, and it refers to a web page that shares information about subjects of interest to the author in much the same way as a journal. Bloggers update their blogs with posts that might be of interest to readers. There are blogs about everything under the sun. Some of the most popular subjects are food, travel, entertainment, animals, and political and public-policy issues.

In the past, all of this information had to be printed in order to reach readers. With a blog, anyone can start writing about anything online and potentially reach a wide audience—if enough people are interested in what the person is writing. As a result, blogging gives writers direct access to readers through the Internet at little or no cost. It has allowed anyone who wants to write or have a voice to try their hand in the Wild West of the writing world. According to *Journalism: A Very Short Introduction* by Ian Hargreaves, Andrew Sullivan, one of the first successful political bloggers, defined a blog as "the first journalistic model that actually harnesses rather than merely exploits the true democratic nature of the web. It's a new medium finally finding a unique voice."

Sullivan made a living writing a blog, receiving payment and a platform for his political commentary. Not all are so lucky. Turning blogging into a career is a difficult feat, but it can be done, and bloggers are a regular part of today's workforce.

Easy Entry

No formal educational requirements are necessary to start plucking away at a personal blog. For in-house jobs, however, a bachelor's degree will likely be required, as well as some kind of proof that you can produce blog posts, most commonly by showing a potential employer your personal blog or entries that you have posted on other people's blogs. Useful majors for college students include journalism, English literature, marketing, and business.

Passion Necessary

The two most important personality traits for blogging are a manic interest in sharing new information through written blog posts and a passion for the topic of your blog. Bloggers are required to be highly productive because new content is what keeps readers interested in the blog. To produce those new blog posts, you will also have to research trends in your field and think creatively about crafting your story. "Skip the generic fill-in-the-blank corporate writing," writes Heidi Cohen in her marketing blog, the *Actionable Marketing Guide*. "It's hard to compose great content if you don't feel strongly about your subject. Think in terms of the words and details you choose. Show your readers why your topic matters to you."

A Tough Way to Make a Living

How one gets paid for blogging is one of the trickiest and most widely discussed questions in the blogging world. The low entry

The Joys of Success

"I never intended to make money as a blogger when I started. It was an experiment aimed solely at gaining more traffic from search engines. Little did I know that my blog would eventually become my business and just a few short years later I'd sell off all my other businesses just to pursue blogging. . . . Today my blog has helped pay for my house, my car, an 8 month trip around the world and I've just purchased a plush two bedroom apartment in my favorite suburb, where I will be moving to next month just before my 30th birthday."

Yaro Starak, "Do You Want to Become a Professional Blogger?," *Entrepreneurs-Journey .com* (blog), 2016. www.entrepreneurs-journey.com.

barrier to starting a blog is what has made blogging so common, but making money has proved elusive for the vast majority of bloggers.

But let's separate the two types of bloggers first. Bloggers who work in-house for companies, online publishers, and non-profits, among other employers, usually get paid and work in the offices along with the rest of the staff. These employees receive a regular salary that will generally fall at the lower end of the pay scale for that particular type of business. Many of these bloggers are younger employees, familiar with technology and social media, and accustomed to chatting in the lingo of the online world. They act as part of the on-staff marketing and public relations of the business or agency that employs them.

Blogging on one's own is a whole other ball game. The Internet is covered with ads boasting of magical paths that lead bloggers to riches, and there are certainly success stories. But most independent bloggers do not make a full-time salary by blogging. Some manage to create steady extra income, and others make little to nothing at all. A few tenacious bloggers manage to turn their passion into a full-time, paying gig.

Darren Rowse, for example, once worked part-time as a minister while working other assorted jobs. Five years after he started his first blog, he was making about $250,000 a year from blogging, according to the *Wall Street Journal*. But Rowse, who currently runs ProBlogger, a popular how-to site for bloggers, points out that this is not the norm and that it took him years to cultivate his blog while making much less money. "I've often used the analogy of Professional sports people to highlight that in any 'game' there are many who play it—less who make a little money from the game, even less who are able to earn a living from it (just) and just a small group who make big money from it," writes Rowse. "The same is true for bloggers."

People who run their own blogs make money in a few different ways. The first and most important is through advertising revenue. Bloggers get paid by a company to host an advertisement on their blog and are generally paid based on the number of people who visit the blog. This has created a pressing need for visitors, sometimes just referred to as "eyeballs" or "clicks." Since growing an audience takes time and a lot of work, making money through advertising can be a slow process, and most blogs fail to reach large enough audiences to result in a full-time salary.

Increasingly, blogs are turning to new methods to make money. These can be link affiliates, such as Amazon. The online bookseller pays a blogger when a blog refers readers to a book on Amazon's website. The affiliate then shares a fraction of the profits made by the sale of a particular product, such as a book in the case of Amazon, with the blogger. Some bloggers also make money by selling original merchandise such as T-shirts and mugs through their blogs.

Who's Hiring?

A 2016 job search for open blogging positions on Indeed, a job-listings website, displayed 1,351 openings for related positions, with 118 of those positions tagged as new. While searching for a blogging job, you will have to keep an open mind about your job title. Aside from openings that used "blogger" in the job title (like fashion blogger), many of the positions displayed in the job search were called something else—social media specialist, freelance writer, content creator, assistant marketing manager. Keep an open mind, try to land an interview, and ask a lot of questions about your actual duties so you will know if there is more to the job than just blogging.

Aside from private companies, most media outlets that have an online site now integrate blogging into their regular journalism. This allows media companies to post news developments and to incorporate different voices into their coverage, such as editorial commentary or citizen journalism (stories written by nonprofessionals).

Most large nonprofit institutions also require someone to create content for blogs and social media outreach. That means museums, charitable institutions, and government institutions also hire bloggers, though they are not always called that. And lastly, there is the possibility, though financially riskier, of simply embarking on a career as your own boss and being your own content provider, business strategist, marketer, and sales department.

Working Conditions Variable

Perhaps the main appeal to blogging is the idea of being your own boss and turning your passions into full-time employment. But because a blog might take a year or longer to start making money, it is more likely that a blogger will spend a considerable amount of time growing a blog while working another job that actually pays the bills. Bloggers universally lament the amount of time that blogging eats up. Blogging might give you a free hand in the content of your blog, but you will still need to get regular blog posts up if you are going to make money blogging. This means constantly coming up with new story ideas, relentlessly researching them, and writing at a quick pace to ensure a stream of new content.

In the meantime, you will have to spend time researching how to grow a blog as a business. In doing so, you will find yourself becoming part marketer, part salesperson. And you will have to balance the amount of time you spend managing your blog as a business with the time it takes to create new content for your blog.

If, however, you work in an office blogging, your job will be a combination of solitary writing and research (since there is often only one in-house blogger or social media specialist on staff) and interaction with the marketing department or a manager in a newsroom or magazine. Blogging for a company, magazine, newspaper, or government agency will require an ability to communicate messages in a collaborative way.

Advancement

Advancement as a blogger can mean one of two things. Bloggers who are self-employed can advance in their careers by growing the readership and revenue sources of their blog. As the blog succeeds, more opportunities for cooperation with other bloggers can open up, lessening the time needed to maintain more than one blog. And as a blog grows in popularity, clients who want to get out their own message through blogging will often

Succeeding by Chance

"You started writing about sports because you love sports (and also, hopefully, writing), so yeah. Keep doing it. . . . All the wise council in the world, however, won't change the fact that the road you (and I) face is incredibly fraught with peril, and even if you do everything right, whether or not you succeed is going to be about luck and being in the right place at the right time. There are incredibly gifted writers who have vanished and people you or I consider awful hacks who have plum gigs, and that's partly due to things totally outside of anyone's control."

Robert Silverman, "An Open Letter to a Young Sports Blogger Looking to Get Paid," Vice Sports, July 28, 2014. https://sports.vice.com.

hire bloggers to help their marketing and public relations. Thus, the blogger can grow beyond being solely a content provider and pursue broader business opportunities.

Bloggers at newspapers and magazines are quite often junior employees and can move into more traditional journalism jobs within the organization for which they blog. In other private companies, a blogger might assist the sales and marketing team to drum up excitement about products and trends. This quite naturally could lead to other positions in sales or marketing.

What Is the Future Outlook for Bloggers?

The future of blogging is uncertain. Some online marketing specialists have already begun to argue that blogging is declining because of the rise of new information-sharing platforms such as Twitter.

This argument, however, is somewhat undercut by two factors: the spread of blogging as a routine communications tool for established companies and institutions, and the sharp rise in the number of blogs. The number of individual blogs on Tumblr, for example, jumped from 17.5 million in 2011 to 276 million in 2016. There are likely to be more changes to the way people share online content in the future. And it is simply impossible to tell what will happen to blogging as a job opportunity.

Find Out More

Association of Food Bloggers
website: http://associationoffoodbloggers.org

The Association of Food Bloggers is an online nonprofit intended to serve the food-blogging community by fostering professional standards and norms for the industry. Its website offers educational resources, restaurant industry news, and practical articles about everyday blogging issues such as how to make money.

Blogger
website: www.blogger.com

Google, best known for its popular search engine, offers a free blogging platform called Blogger. It is highly popular with new bloggers because of the ease of use. To use this platform, however, you will need an e-mail account offered by Gmail, which is a free e-mail service from Google.

International Bloggers' Association
website: www.internationalbloggersassociation.com

The International Bloggers' Association is an online association that provides useful information and support services to individual bloggers. There is content both for members, who pay an annual fee, and for nonmembers. Much of the information is intended to help bloggers reach a larger audience.

Professional Travel Bloggers Association
website: http://travelbloggersassociation.com

The Professional Travel Bloggers Association is a membership-based online community of travel bloggers, run by travel bloggers for travel bloggers. Its goal is to turn travel blogging into a unique and profitable profession. It helps connect bloggers with employers and offers content to help bloggers develop professional strategies.

WordPress
website: www.wordpress.com

WordPress is an online hosting site for blogs. It represents about 25 percent of the websites on the Internet. Its website allows users to create free blogs and guides them through the process step-by-step. It also offers advanced services for membership fees.

Grant Writer

A Few Facts

Pay

The average pay for a grant writer in 2014 was $44,000.

Experience Matters

Earnings for grant writers increase with experience.

Education

The minimum degree requirement for grant writers is a bachelor's degree.

Formal Training

Grant-writing programs can be helpful but are not strictly necessary for landing a job.

Job Satisfaction

The majority of grant writers report a high degree of work satisfaction.

What Does a Grant Writer Do?

A grant writer performs a specialized function essential to the operating of nonprofit organizations such as museums, charities, animal rights groups, organizations that provide free medical services, and many other enterprises. In general, these groups don't have many ways to make money. They neither sell products nor charge fees for services. How then do they drum up the money it takes to carry out their missions? One method is through donations, either from regular people or from businesses and other organizations.

A second method is by applying for funding from donor institutions, including government agencies, private corporations, and private foundations. These institutions set aside a vast pool of money to donate (through "grants") to nonprofit organizations that they deem worthy of supporting. In order to tap into that funding, a nonprofit organization will file an extensive application, generally known as a grant proposal—and this is where the grant writer comes in. The grant writer acts as the matchmaker between funders and applicants, deciding which funding

Daily Grind

"10:00 a.m.: Dive into a new grant proposal. I keep a master grants calendar to juggle all my clients and make sure I'm on top of each organization's funding plans. I don't want to miss any deadlines! Around mid- to late morning, I'm fully awake and ready to tackle some tougher projects, like starting a new proposal. This generally entails some heavy research into the funding organization and taking a look at my past grant proposals. I'll write some new language specific for this opportunity and spruce up any old language."

Megan Hill, "A Day in the Life of a Professional Grant Writer," Professional Grant Writers, November 9, 2011. http://professionalgrantwriter.org.

opportunities best fit the organization for which they are writing a grant application. It is the grant writer's job to fill out these applications and try to secure funding for an employer.

In general, grant applications will request all sorts of information about a nonprofit organization, including explanations of its mission, past performance, future plans, and how it spends its money. This information is used by the donor institution to determine if it wants to contribute money to support a particular nonprofit organization.

So far, the process sounds pretty humdrum, and one might ask why anyone would want to make a living filling out forms. But the most important part of the grant application is still to come—the compelling essay that helps convince a funder that the goals of a nonprofit are worth supporting. And here's where the writing really comes in. In general, a successful grant application will be written in concise, well-crafted language. But even more importantly, it will have to build a case, one sentence at a time, for why a nonprofit's mission matches the mission of the funding source—why, in other words, a particular nonprofit is deserving of a grant. In this light, grant writing is a remarkably challenging exercise in persuasive writing.

Since corporations, government agencies, and private institutions all set aside money to fund nonprofit causes, you might also ask just what is so difficult about getting hold of the money. The answer is that getting a grant is highly competitive. There are many nonprofit organizations seeking funding for their particular cause. It is the job of the grant writer to convince the funding source of the merits of a particular project, whether it is to save wetlands, feed the homeless, provide access to medical care to impoverished areas, or fund the arts. These causes all spark passions in different people differently. Some think one goal is more important than another. It is the grant writer's job to convince a donor that one particular cause trumps other causes competing for the same source of funding, and they do this by writing a grant application.

No Special Training Needed

Most grant writers hold at least a bachelor's degree. Commonly studied subjects include English literature, marketing, and public policy, but there is no direct pathway into the field. A growing number of professional certification programs are available for grant writers that offer a stamp of professional approval. These are not strictly necessary, however, and many grant writers secure jobs without obtaining certification. "Grant writers are not hired on a degree status nor does the field require advanced training and, more times than not, the person assigned the task may not have been formally trained at all," explains Vanessa S. O'Neal, founder of the National Society of Grant Writing Professionals, in the article "The Truth About Grant Writing Certification." She adds, "According to professional standards, a grant writer does not have to be professionally trained to occupy the position."

Caring About Your Cause

Although you don't need a particular degree to land a job as a grant writer, you will need to know how to write well. For grant writing, this means being able to marshal arguments to convince a donor to support your cause. It also means being highly detail oriented and being able to manage a complicated process while working with others.

Beyond these skills, there is the question of personality. Successful grant writers argue that grant writing can be done most effectively when the author cares as much about a cause as the organization that employs the grant writer. Grant writing, therefore, attracts people who are passionate about the world around them, specific causes, and making a difference by finding funding for those causes. "At its heart, fundraising is helping others connect an existing passion directly to your cause," writes Marc Koenig in the 2014 article "7 Tips on Asking for Donations—It's Intimidating, We Get It." He adds, "We don't convince donors. We help them realize that they already care."

Ways to Make Money

PayScale, an online site that tracks wage data, estimates that the median annual income for grant writers is $44,000 a year, and its research shows a close link between the number of years of experience and higher pay rates. Senior grant writers or directors of nonprofit development, both more senior positions, average about $63,000 per year, according to PayScale. Many grant writers, especially freelance grant writers, also bill by the hour, and rates can vary from $20 to $100 per hour, according to anecdotal evidence collected by the Bureau of Labor Statistics.

Finding the Right Fit

Finding a job as a grant writer is easiest if you match your interests with an organization that cares about the same issues. A search conducted in January 2016 on Indeed, a job-hunting website, revealed 810 job openings for grant writers. They ranged from educational services to institutions that provide housing assistance to food banks and health care outreach. Your best strategy is to apply to the jobs that focus on issues you care most about.

Grant writers are generally hired in one of three ways. Some organizations hire full-time staff writers to oversee their grant applications. Others hire grant writers for specific projects, and grant writers can make a livable salary by cobbling together different clients, often in the same field, while working from home but with frequent meetings to strategize on the grant applications. The third pool of jobs can be found in consulting companies that hire staff members to serve the grant-writing needs of various clients. For the grant writer, these companies offer stable employment and access to the established business relationships between the agency and its clients.

A Day in the Life

Grant writing is a process that involves some routine steps. Whether you are working freelance or directly for an institution in their offices, you will likely start the grant-writing process by consulting with the executive director or the head of grant writing to explore possible funding sources. This will be followed by some research into those funding sources. Major donors such as the Alfred P. Sloan Foundation, a US philanthropic organization,

Get to the Point

"Keep in mind, traffic on the 'fundraising highway' is intense and growing in volume. If you receive a 'no,' think of ways to turn that response into a 'yes' the next time you apply. The increase in requests for nonprofit support also means you should get to the point in your cover letter. Do not bury your urgent case for support in the text, as your proposal may find itself in a large stack of similar documents on the desk of the potential donor — try to 'stand out.'"

Carolyn M. Appleton, "Grant Writing: A Reality Check," *Carolyn's Nonprofit Blog*. http://carolynmappleton.com.

give clear guidelines for the application process. The organization's website even spells out what kinds of things the foundation doesn't fund, such as individuals or for-profit organizations. This research will be invaluable in targeting your funding sources, and much of your time will be spent thoroughly researching funding institutions before you can start on the grant-writing process.

Once you get to the grant-writing phase of the process, you will need to further consult with your employer to round up all the essential information—how the money will be spent, what concrete goals the organization has achieved, how many people the funding will impact and in what ways. Being as specific as possible is a sure way for your application to receive a favorable response. Finally, there is the writing of the essay or proposal section of the application, in which you make the main arguments for why your organization deserves a pile of free money from an outside donor. This is the portion of the application where you put your writing skills to work and convince donors that their money would achieve the best results in advancing a cause through your employer's programs.

Advancement

A grant writer is something of a specialist in the world of writing—performing a specific function separate from other functions in the foundation that employs him or her. This might suggest that the position offers little room for advancement. But because grant writers work closely with executive directors and other leaders of nonprofit organizations to strategize for new funding campaigns, they often have a variety of skills that make them an integral part of an organization's executive team. It is not unusual for grant writers to move into managerial roles, such as a director of grants position, at nonprofit organizations. In this role, they can direct strategies to help achieve the core mission of the nonprofit group. There is, therefore, considerable room to advance one's career as a grant writer or to transition into other aspects of nonprofit and fund-raising work.

What Is the Future Outlook for Grant Writers?

Anecdotal evidence indicates that the employment outlook for grant writers is uncertain. While some grant writers praise the growing professionalism of their field, others lament the consolidation of grant-writing professionals, which essentially squeezes out less-experienced grant writers. Others complain about the bureaucratic obstacles to tapping into funding that flows through federal and state government agencies. Yet there are still plenty of private foundations that both seek and award grants, and they regularly hire grant writers to help them through the funding process.

Grant writing is also subject to larger economic pressures. When the economy slows down or a charitable institution's resources dip because of a sluggish stock market, then the awarding of grants slows down. This can cause swings in the job opportunities for grant writers and undermine stable employment. But the number of jobs listed on job-search sites suggests that there is still plenty of opportunity to land a job as a grant writer.

Find Out More

American Grant Writers' Association
235 Apollo Beach Blvd., #318
Apollo Beach, FL 33572
phone: (813) 260-3304
website: www.agwa.us

The American Grant Writers' Association is a professional association for grant writers that promotes professionalism and ethical standards in grant writing. It also offers educational programs such as including online courses, seminars, and webinars through its website.

Association of Fundraising Professionals

4300 Wilson Blvd., Suite 300
Arlington, VA 22203
phone: (703) 684-0410
website: www.afpnet.org

The Association of Fundraising Professionals is an umbrella organization covering many aspects of the fund-raising field, including grant writing. The association welcomes young professionals and has resources for career development on its website.

Grant Professionals Association

10881 Lowell Ave., Suite 190
Overland Park, KS 66210
phone: (913) 788-3000
website: www.grantprofessionals.org

The Grant Professionals Association is a professional organization founded by grant writers to promote their craft. It has more than eighteen hundred members. The association promotes communication in the grant-writing community through conferences and advocates for certification standards for grant-writing professionals. Its website also includes links to the association's publications, including the annual *GPA Journal*.

Society for Nonprofit Organizations

PO Box 510354
Livonia, MI 48151
phone: (734) 451-3582
website: www.snpo.org

The Society for Nonprofit Organizations has more than six thousand members and seeks to enhance knowledge about the nonprofit sector. Its website features links to free resources, including fund-raising guides, articles, and book reviews. The website also features a jobs section and a link to the society's publication, *Nonprofit World*.

Advertising and Marketing

What Jobs Can Writers Do in Advertising and Marketing?

Advertising and marketing are linked but not quite the same. Advertising is a more specific activity within the marketing process. It generally refers to the production of information about products or services that are intended to spark interest among new customers. Marketing is the broader strategy for promoting goods or services through a range of activities, including advertising.

The most writing-heavy part of the marketing process is the crafting of advertising copy. This is the writing of the actual text that will be featured in magazine ads, television commercials, billboards, and increasingly, on computer screens and smartphones. A writer cannot produce ad copy, however, without first understanding the goals of an overall marketing campaign. What is the ad trying to say? Who is the target audience? What words and images would best fit the ad campaign?

A 1994 magazine ad for a Motorola mobile phone, for example, depicted a clunky, battered walkie-talkie used

Jugglers Wanted

"My responsibilities vary every day. . . . On any given day, I am writing content, creating a strategy deck, posting for a client on Facebook, taking photos at an event for social posting, and I'm in meetings, meetings, and more meetings. It requires flexibility and it requires agility. You have to be prepared to juggle a lot of different things at once and you have to be prepared to do many different jobs. From day to day, I am doing work related to every role in this company (as are my coworkers)—that's the nature of an agency."

Jenna Britton, quoted in Louisa Wells, "Career Profiles: Digital Marketing Manager Jenna Britton," *The Everygirl* (blog), 2016. http://theeverygirl.com.

by US soldiers during World War II. Next to it was a sleek new Motorola mobile phone. The ad copy read: "Daddy fought in the war." In smaller type, the copywriter played up the themes of reliability, tradition, and innovation to create a favorable impression of the company and its products. Words in advertising and marketing are used to wrap a product in a story—a heroic past and an innovative future, in the case of the Motorola advertisement. The writer must therefore be highly innovative and rely on imagination to create a concept and story line that will be expressed in concise ad copy, sometimes no more than a few lines long.

Increasingly, advertising and marketing specialists work in the digital world. Two factors are driving this: People spend more time on computers and smartphones, and the possibilities for advertisements are almost unlimited in this new arena. An online ad can pop up, vanish, and be replaced by another one in the blink of an eye. Digital ads are featured on online news sites, just as they are in printed newspapers, and they are a regular part of many of the applications we use and web pages we visit. This technological change has made digital advertising and marketing the fastest-growing part of the industry and created jobs that did not exist before. A digital marketing specialist, for example, will need to be able to produce ad copy, direct mailings, and other advertising and marketing content entirely in a virtual world.

The rapid expansion of desktop computing and mobile smartphones has also created an entirely new marketing job. This is the social media specialist. As part of the marketing team, and perhaps even a copywriter by training, a social media specialist helps promote products and services by writing about them on social media sites. This means writing tweets on Twitter, posting messages on Facebook and Instagram, and keeping abreast of the newest social media sites for new opportunities as the faddish world of social media changes. Aside from posting on social media, social media specialists also write up new content on a daily basis for blogs that are directly associated with the product, a range of products, or the company that makes them.

Seventy-eight percent of companies now use social media for marketing, according to Sprout Social, a social marketing consultancy. "It's time to do away with the old mindset and outdated views of marketing," writes Dominique Jackson, a digital

An ad agency team works out their strategy for a new ad campaign. They'll write up the plan and craft ads for different types of media, depending on who they want to reach.

marketing specialist, in "Using Social Media for Business Growth in 2015." She adds, "The Internet has completely changed the way your business has to look at marketing. And social media is the perfect example of this shift."

Educational Qualifications

A bachelor's degree is generally required for entry-level positions, and many colleges now offer degrees in advertising and marketing. It is not necessary, however, to have majored in the subject. People with various educational backgrounds have found their way into the profession, including those who majored in literature, communications, history, art, and business.

Social Butterflies Wanted

The advertising and marketing workplace is a highly social environment. People who like working on group projects might be a natural fit. It is also essential to be a highly detail-oriented person who can follow through on the many collaborative changes that will come up through the process of creating a marketing campaign. Employers have also come to demand good social media skills, so if you find yourself constantly sharing things you like on Twitter, Facebook, and Instagram, your employer will likely want to put those habits to work in a marketing campaign.

Working on a marketing campaign also demands a combination of creativity and business acumen. While managers and marketing strategists often handle the business side of the equation, copywriters, illustrators, and art directors also need a good head for business. They simply can't create effective advertisements without first understanding the overall business targets. And copywriters measure their own job performance through concrete indicators of a campaign's success, such as sales figures and the number of potential customers an ad campaign reaches.

Potential for Pay Growth

PayScale, a company that tracks wages, estimates that an advertising copywriter earned a median income of $46,000 per year as of January 2016. But because of the many routes to advancement, there is a high potential for salary growth. A senior copywriter, for example, made an average salary of about $71,000 per year as of January 2016, according to PayScale. Further advancement to a position as an advertising, promotions, or marketing manager will lead to another jump in pay. In 2014 the average median income for these managers was $123,450 per year, according to the Bureau of Labor Statistics (BLS).

In High Demand

In an economy driven by consumers purchasing goods and services, it shouldn't be surprising that there is a high demand for advertising and marketing specialists who help companies convince consumers to choose specific brands. A search for advertising and marketing openings on Indeed, a job-listings website, at the beginning of 2016 revealed a whopping thirty-seven thousand jobs across the United States, with more than two thousand recently added listings. A search just for copywriters showed more than thirty-four hundred job openings.

The diversity of employers, in part, drives these numbers. About 31 percent of advertising and promotions managers worked for advertising agencies in 2014, according to the BLS. That means that the majority of jobs are actually found outside of traditional advertising agencies. Large companies like Nike or Apple will often have large teams on staff to handle advertising and marketing. Even small companies often have a few employees who handle social media marketing and coordinate with outside ad agencies. In other words, jobs in this field can be found nearly everywhere, from law firms to manufacturers to consulting companies and environmental groups.

Work Life

Advertising and marketing people generally work in an office, either for an agency or consulting company with external clients or for a company that provides goods or services. These specialists' jobs are collaborative, with input coming from managers, clients, and coworkers. Constant interaction, frequent deadlines, and the need for instant creativity create something of a pressure-cooker environment. "Marketing can be like trying to change a tire while driving down the freeway in a high-speed chase," marketing coach Veronika Noize explained to *Forbes* magazine. "Truly challenging, exhilarating, and not for the faint of heart."

An average day might start with a strategy meeting, followed by some brainstorming for an ad campaign or new marketing strategy. A copywriter will work closely with someone from the art department to coordinate the written and visual elements of an ad, either digital or print. Various people in the process might share open files on a different computer to test the look of an online advertisement. The copywriter and other members of the creative team will also work closely with computer specialists, usually in the production department, to make sure the technical specifications for online or mobile marketing are workable. Inevitably, more meetings will follow. Managers—and perhaps even clients—will give input. And round it goes, until the ad finally goes to print or is posted online.

At the same time, members of the marketing team constantly update social media sites, blogs, and perhaps craft messages for direct e-mailing as part of the overall marketing strategy. They might also write up the text for posters for a promotional event or a script for a TV ad promoting their product or service.

Movin' On Up

The sky's the limit with opportunities for career advancement in advertising and marketing. Junior copywriters can advance to become senior copywriters or manage a copy department. But

Communication Is Key

"You would think that in the communications business that everyone would be great communicators. . . . When I was running my own digital shop I quickly realized that I had to rethink the way I wrote emails to clients and partners. When trying to get to the point in emails, the recipient would sometimes call back wondering if I was upset because they took my tone as being assertive. This was never the case. I've since tried to adjust the way I get to the point and it has resulted in happy clients and colleagues. Email is typically the most frequently used communication tool at an Advertising Agency."

Ross Simmonds, "How to Survive & Thrive at an Advertising Agency—My Guide," *Ross Simmonds* (blog), 2016. http://rosssimmonds.com.

because copywriters and all other advertising and marketing people work so closely as a team, they also learn the basics of each other's jobs. This can mean considerable room to change positions within a marketing department and to take over higher-paying managerial functions.

Because there are so many advertising and marketing jobs in different industries, there is plenty of opportunity for career advancement by looking for a new job at a different company. Jumping ship sometimes leads to rapid advances up the career ladder, though employers are sometimes wary of employees who have not held a job for at least a few years.

What Is the Future Outlook for Jobs in Advertising and Marketing?

Because advertising and marketing are rapidly adapting to technological changes, data about job growth are conflicting. According to the BLS, for example, jobs for writers, including advertising copywriters, are expected to grow at 2 percent between 2014 and 2024. That is a growth rate slower than the national average and suggests that copywriters will face tough competition for jobs in the future.

In its projections for advertising, promotions, or marketing managers (the people who manage copywriters), the BLS expects these jobs to grow at 9 percent between 2014 and 2024, a rate much faster than the national average. How can this discrepancy be explained? One explanation is that the job title of advertising copywriters is changing as the result of more advertising and marketing moving onto digital platforms. They are often called "digital marketing specialists" or "creative content providers." Their jobs will incorporate technological know-how and work on a digital platform. This is a significant change for a copywriter used to working in a print medium. But growth in digital advertising and marketing jobs should track more closely with the growth of management, making it a fast-growing field with plenty of potential.

Find Out More

American Advertising Federation
1101 Vermont Ave. NW, Suite 500
Washington, DC 20005
phone: (202) 898-0089
website: www.aaf.org

The American Advertising Federation is a professional trade association for the advertising industry. It represents about forty thousand professionals, including sixty-five hundred student members. In the interest of furthering excellence in the field, the association sponsors a national student advertising competition and summer camps for students interested in a career in the field.

American Marketing Association
130 E. Randolph St., 22nd Floor
Chicago, IL 60601
phone: (312) 542-9000
website: www.ama.org

The American Marketing Association is the largest professional group for the industry in the United States. Its website features information on the state of the profession, links to jobs, and a career resource center for students, as well as webinars and information about seminars.

eMarketing Association (eMA)
40 Blue Ridge Dr.
Charlestown, RI 02813
phone: (800) 496-2950
website: www.emarketingassociation.com

The eMA is the largest association for online marketing, a fast-growing aspect of the profession. The group also offers certification in aspects of online marketing, and the website features career information and links as well as some statistical information on the growth of digital marketing.

Social Media Club (SMC)
PO Box 14881
San Francisco, CA 94114-0881
website: https://socialmediaclub.org

The SMC is a nonprofit membership community for global networking among digital professionals, including digital marketers and advertisers. Its website features a blog with posts on the changing nature of digital media, as well as a career resource center and information about seminars and events in the field.

Communications and Public Relations

What Does a Communications and Public Relations Specialist Do?

At its most basic, the function of a communications and public relations (PR) specialist is to craft a positive message on behalf of an organization. This might be a private corporation, such as an oil company or a bank, or a nonprofit organization, such as a medical center or university. The government also employs PR specialists to help explain public policy decisions and to inform citizens of the services that the government performs on their behalf. The PR specialist therefore acts as a bridge between an organization and the segments of the public that the organization hopes to reach with a particular message.

The duties of PR specialists are broad, since they use many different ways to reach the public and to craft an image or message for their employers. Because of the many tasks involved, a PR specialist generally works on a specific PR campaign—a concerted series of activities intended to get out a message. A PR campaign will generally include several steps, many of

Doing Whatever It Takes

"It's a far cry from the career I had in my mind's eye. I was delivering four foot high helium balloons to journalists, carving out articles from the paper with a scalpel and using PritStick to mount it on paper and stuffing media kits with interminable releases, executive bios and product spec sheets. Oh the glamour of it all. . . . Along with all of this I do what people call 'account management' basically making [sure] everything about a project goes smoothly and that the client is happy."

Ed Lee, "So, Public Relations . . . What DO You Do All Day?," *The Blog Herald*, April 13, 2007. www.blogherald.com.

which involve writing, that are intended to address different audiences and to reach the greatest number of people in the target audience.

In 2016, for example, the US Department of Energy (DOE) decided to end federal subsidies and tax breaks for solar energy. The solar energy subsidies helped make the technology cheaper and more competitive with other energy sources, like coal, which is more harmful to the environment. The subsidies helped boost solar production and cut solar energy costs for consumers. A change in the policy would therefore impact many different groups. As part of the DOE's PR campaign to explain the change in policy, PR specialists issued press releases to news organizations to explain why the DOE was ending subsidies and fielded questions from the media over the rationale for the new policy and its possible effects on individuals and solar manufacturers. The PR campaign also included postings on Facebook, Twitter, and other social media platforms both to inform people of the changes and to measure public response to the change in policy. PR specialists also wrote speeches for DOE officials who were called on to explain the policy change.

A PR campaign for a private employer would look much the same as this government PR campaign, but it might also include promotional events to drum up interest in the sale of goods or services. As a result, the PR department of a private company quite often works closely with its advertising and marketing team.

No Need for a PhD

An entry-level position as a communications and PR specialist generally requires a bachelor's degree. Related majors in college are media and mass communications, public relations, English literature, business, or marketing. It is also not uncommon to have a master's degree in a related field, though it is not strictly necessary.

Most importantly, you will need to be good at communicating to different audiences in a variety of ways. "A major service you provide in your professional environment is communications counseling," explained Marisa Ellison, communications manager at the Missouri Department of Transportation, in her 2016 webinar "Communications Counseling—Step by Step." She added, "No need for a Ph.D. . . . just the know-how to help your agency understand the importance of communication and what it can do to help get work done more easily, efficiently, and effectively."

Doing It All

Effective writing is essential for success as a communications and PR specialist, and there is a good deal of psychology involved too. "A great PR professional is a great writer that understands human nature," explained Betsy Hays, who teaches PR in the Department of Mass Communication and Journalism at California State University–Fresno, in an interview with the *SmartRecruiters* blog. "They have beautiful intuition and can articulate their ideas in a clear, concise way."

Interpersonal skills are also highly valued, since you will be dealing with the public and with clients. So is the ability to write a speech and deliver a presentation. And there will be constant phone contact and the updating of social media. All of this takes a great deal of organization, and one of the most frequently heard demands made of PR specialists is that they stay on message—that they use all of the communications channels for a very specific end.

Unlike many writing jobs, the PR specialist will also be required to put out fires when they arise. A government agency might be getting bad press because of a new policy, and the PR department will shift into overdrive to help counter the negative press by spinning a message in a more favorable light. The job is most highly suited, therefore, to outgoing people who like to have a lot on their plate. It is one of the most interactive and collaborative of all jobs that rely heavily on writing.

Pay

The median annual pay for a PR specialist in 2014 was $55,680, according to the Bureau of Labor Statistics (BLS). Salaries range according to the industry that employs the specialist, with professional, scientific, and technical fields paying higher salaries; and educational, health care, and social assistance organizations ranking toward the lower end. PayScale, a company that tracks wages, shows modest potential for salary increases with promotion. A PR manager, for example, had a median annual income of $61,193 in January 2016, while a corporate communications manager had an annual income of $75,126. Directors of PR departments earned an even higher median salary at $81,212.

No Shortage of Jobs

Communications and PR jobs are plentiful. There are dedicated PR firms that hire specialists who then work for clients on particular PR campaigns. And there are also PR specialists who work directly for large organizations, both public and private. If you imagine that every company, nonprofit organization, and government agency wants to promote a positive image of its work, you will get a sense of just how many employers are out there. A search in early 2016 on Indeed, an employment website, showed more than 178,000 job openings for corporate communications alone.

Of those, nearly 11,000 had been listed recently. The employers included major banks, pharmaceutical companies, and private educational enterprises.

A search for PR jobs at the same time showed more than sixty-five thousand openings and included nonprofit organizations, universities, and government agencies. Remember that when you are searching for openings in this field, you will need to use a few different search terms, such as "public relations," "communications specialist," and "social media specialist."

Long Days

One of the most common complaints about communications and PR work is that it is hectic. This can mean working long hours in a stressful environment. It might not be at all clear when the day will end, and working on weekends is also common.

A typical day might start with catching up on news or feedback from previous PR campaigns, checking e-mails from clients and the media, and answering all immediate questions from clients and managers. The next step will likely be an internal meeting with others from the PR department and executives from the company or organization to strategize on PR activities and run through progress on various aspects of the campaign. The PR specialist might then write up new press releases, make calls to the media, draft some copy for a brochure or pamphlet, update social media sites, and generally bang out some of the writing copy that is so important to a PR campaign.

An afternoon might include a meeting with clients or an event intended to drum up business. That might be followed by drafting or revising a speech for an executive or government official and attending an event where the speech will be delivered. The work of the PR specialist doesn't end there: he or she might continue to work with media contacts to help shape the impression of the event. These events quite often fall on weekends or in the evening, when people have time to get out of their offices to attend.

If this sounds like a lot to do in a day, most PR specialists would probably agree with you. "Agency life in the PR world is not for the timid or the dull—or those dependent upon eight hours of sleep a night," writes PR specialist Kellie Bramlet in her article "The Life of a PR Agency Employee" on the news website *Ragan's PR Daily*. "Agency life is for the bold, the creative, and the smartphone-addicted."

Advancement

There is considerable room for advancement in the communications and PR fields. There is room both for vertical advancement (a promotion) and lateral movement (moving to a similar job at another company). An entry-level job in a PR department or even as a social media specialist can lead to promotions to PR manager (who manages campaigns and perhaps other PR specialists) and eventually to PR director, who oversees the department. The same is true for corporate communications and government PR work. Advancement is also possible by acquiring skills and then shopping for a related job in the field at another place of employment. Because of the vast number of employers, moving between jobs can often lead to more rapid promotion in a good job market.

Future Outlook for PR Jobs

PR jobs are expected to grow 6 percent through 2024, according to the BLS. This is about as fast as the national average and indicates that competition for jobs will remain strong. Technology is changing PR jobs, which rely increasingly on new platforms to reach the public, including social media. But there is no reason to believe that demand for PR specialists will flag anytime soon.

Find Out More

International Association of Business Communicators (IABC)
155 Montgomery St., Suite 1210
San Francisco, CA 94104
phone: (415) 544-4700
website: www.iabc.com

The IABC offers courses in professional development and information about networking events. The association's website also features career information, industry news, podcasts, and articles pertaining to aspects of public relations.

International Public Relations Association (IPRA)
Suite 5879
PO Box 6945
London, England W1A 6US
phone: +44 1634 818308
website: www.ipra.org

The IPRA fosters contact among public relations specialists around the globe. The organization's website contains information about trends in the field, future conferences, and information about the group's current campaigns, such as its campaign for media transparency.

National Association of Government Communicators (NAGC)
201 Park Washington Ct.
Falls Church, VA 22046-4527
phone: (703) 538-1787
website: www.nagc.com

The NAGC is a national nonprofit professional association for communications specialists working for state and federal government agencies. It acts as a professional resource for government communications specialists and fosters exchanges within the community.

National Communication Association (NCA)
1765 N St. NW
Washington, DC 20036
phone: (202) 464-4622
website: www.natcom.org

The NCA is a leading academic advocate for the study of communication as an academic discipline. It publishes several academic journals on the field and monitors data on related trends. It also maintains a career center to help place communications students.

Public Relations Society of America (PRSA)
33 Maiden Ln., 11th Floor
New York, NY 10038-5150
phone: (212) 460-1400
website: www.prsa.org

The PRSA is the oldest and largest public relations professional association in the United States. The group encourages professional development, ethical standards, and continuing education in the field. It also mentors students though the Public Relations Student Society of America. The PRSA website contains a career services section as well.

Screenwriter

What Does a Screenwriter Do?

A screenwriter develops a script for adaptation to visual productions, such as movies, TV shows, and video games. It is one writing form where the words pecked out by the author provide only the raw material—the story line, characters, and dialogue—for further creative use by a filmmaker, TV director, or video game creator. As a result, screenwriting demands that the author keep in mind the needs of the person who will eventually make use of the script. "The great thing about screenwriting is that it's easy to get started," said Matt McNevin, a screenwriting teacher, in a 2013 interview with the BLS *Occupational Outlook Quarterly*. "All you need is a pen and paper." But he points out that it is probably quite an alien form of writing and takes some practice. "Learning to write a screenplay is like learning a new language," he says.

That new language is one that will work on film. It is generally driven by dialogue, since the descriptive writing in a novel or other creative work will largely be provided by the director, cinematographer, and others involved in making a film. The screenwriter, in fact, provides just the first, but vital, step in a long process that will result in the transformation of the written word into a visual creation for the entertainment industry.

Finding Creative Inspiration

A screenwriter generally relies on two types of inspiration when starting the process of writing a screenplay. The first is his or her own imagination, crafting an original script in much the same way that a novelist thinks up a new story. The second is the adaptation—the reworking of a novel, play, comic book, old movie, or historical event into a new script designed to be produced on film or TV.

If the script is original, the screenwriter will need to think up characters, a plotline, and most importantly, dialogue from scratch. If the script is an adaptation of a novel, play, or comic book, the screenwriter will first need to secure the legal rights to rework the script for film or TV. This is generally done by a TV or film studio. Once the rights are secured, the screenwriter will work closely with a director or producer to craft a vision for the final product. This will likely require a succession of meetings with producers and directors and a whole team of developers, followed by crafting the first draft of a script. In all likelihood, the first draft will attract a barrage of criticism and requests for changes. The screenwriter then goes back and redrafts the script until the final product is something that the studio feels it can work with.

In the case of an adaptation of a historical event, the screenwriter will begin by researching the subject matter, scouring books on the topic, visiting archives to examine historical records, and consulting experts in the field. The screenwriter will essentially begin the project the same way that a historian would begin researching a book. But once the writing starts, the screenwriter will engage in a very different form of writing than the historian. Much of the screenwriter's focus will fall on the search for a story line and characters that can be adapted to film or TV. The historical narrative will serve only the purpose of telling a story for

Thick Skin Needed

"I will not disclose the name of the studio, but it really doesn't matter which one it is, because the only thing that changes most of the time is the brand of bottled water I cling to as my hope for getting my script made is pried from the realm of the possible. If this sounds depressing, well, that's because it is. There's a multiplex in my mind where the unmade movies on my computer are showing nightly. The studio validates my parking if not my ideas."

Lesley Suter and Taffy Brodesser-Akner, "A Day in the Life of a Screenwriter," *Condé Nast Traveler*, February 10, 2011. www.cntraveler.com.

entertainment purposes, no matter how faithfully the screenwriter sticks to the facts. Ultimately, the screenwriter is in search of a piece of writing that is very different in both purpose and style from that of a historian.

With the explosion of video games since the 1980s, screenwriters today also work on developing characters and story lines for this entirely new realm of screenwriting. Screenwriting for video games, however, is distinct from other types of screenwriting in that it is highly collaborative from the beginning. The video game writer first meets with a technical team of game developers to see what stories, actions, and dialogue will work with the technical specifications of a video game. The screenwriter will then work with the game developers each step of the way as they create the game, filling in new bits of action and dialogue as the developers come up with workable technology for an interactive game.

Practice, Practice, Practice

Most screenwriters have obtained at least a bachelor's degree, often in writing or literature. Some also attend master's programs for creative writing or earn a master's degree in fine arts in screenwriting. Beyond a love of writing, screenwriting takes practice, often by writing script after script, until a screenwriter hones the craft and learns to write for the unique specifications of film or TV. "Screenwriting, like any other form of professional writing, is a specific, learnable craft that requires study, talent, training, practice and an immense level of commitment," explains Michael Hauge, a script consultant and screenwriting teacher, in an article on the Writers Store website.

Living with Rejection

The mention of screenwriting inspires fantasies of fame and glamour. What writer wouldn't like to see his or her work adapted to a Hollywood blockbuster or a hit TV show? But the reality is that most scripts meet with a firm "no." Rejection is part of the process, and the screenwriter must get used to returning to the drawing board to meet the ever-changing demands of his or her employer. "If executives think your script will advance their career, they'll like you," writes scriptwriter Karl Iglesias in "The Six Essential Habits of Highly Successful Screenwriters." He adds, "If they don't, they'll ignore you. If you can't handle these inconsistencies psychologically, [you] set yourself up for major frustrations and depression." Although the screenwriter will often work for periods in creative isolation, this back-and-forth will require interpersonal skills to keep the collaborative process moving in a positive direction.

The Big Bucks Are Out There but Only for a Lucky Few

Writing a Hollywood movie or a successful TV show often brings visions of dollar signs. Scripts have sold for more than $3 million, but this is the exception, not the rule. Ken Miyamoto, a screenwriter, compares it to winning the lottery. "Those are lottery type numbers to behold," he writes in *ScreenCraft*, an industry publication. "Those deals are very similar to the lottery—but not as one would hope. . . . It would be silly for anyone to invest their time and money expecting to win the lottery, right? The same could be said for screenwriters expecting to join the six or seven figure club."

More often the pay range for a script is between $5,000 and $200,000, and more often than not it falls toward the lower end. Payment is often made in two parts. The first is the original purchase of the script from the screenwriter, often for half the amount. The second half is then paid only if the movie is actually made, which could take years if it ever happens at all. In terms of pay, it is a hit-or-miss business, and most screenwriters struggle to make ends meet. PayScale, a company that tracks salaries, put the median annual salary at $42,500 in early 2016.

Who's Hiring?

The enormous growth of the entertainment industry over the past fifty years might lead one to assume that screenwriters are in high demand. But this is not quite so. A single successful screenwriter can handle a succession of projects for a movie studio or a TV series. The trick, it seems, is breaking in—meeting the right people and catching a break. There is an old joke that everyone in Hollywood is an actor, from your waiter to your hairdresser, and the same could be said of screenwriters. Many end up scraping out a living doing other kinds of work while they wait for their big break. "They discover that it's not just about great writing," says Ken Miyamoto in an article on the website Quora about out-of-work screenwriters. "They learn that it takes networking. They learn that it likely means moving to Los Angeles. They learn that their beloved scripts are often calling cards to writing assignments and will likely never be produced."

In short, entry into the profession of screenwriting is difficult. And while there are screenwriters typing out all those TV shows and movies that entertain Americans on a daily basis, it can be difficult to know just how to join the ranks of professional screenwriters. A 2016 search on Indeed, a job-hunting website, revealed a paltry total of twenty-four screenwriting jobs, with only three listed recently. But online job advertisements are not really how screenwriters find work. It takes connections, pounding the pavement, and a lot of luck.

Work Life

If you are lucky enough to find a job as a screenwriter, you will certainly have a lot of flexibility in your work life. Aside from meetings with producers and directors at the initial phase, most screenwriters can work where they please, either from home or from a coffee shop or library. Rewrites may force them back into an office, but in general it is a profession that focuses more on the finished product than on routine cycles of office life. To pay the bills, however, it is very common for all but the most successful screenwriters to have a second job, either editing or doing other types of writing—or just waiting tables. As a result of the financial pressures, some of the freedom of being able to work from home will be eaten up by regular shifts doing other jobs that will allow a screenwriter to earn enough money to keep writing.

Success Elusive, but Possible

Screenwriters can achieve a good reputation with a few successful screenplays, and for those lucky enough to do so, prospects for work can improve. A small number of screenwriters even become somewhat famous in their own right. For most screenwriters, however, it is a slog, pumping out script after script until they find some success. Moreover, there is very little room for advancement, since the other jobs at movie studios, TV networks, and video game companies generally require very different skills. A screenwriter is essentially embarking on a make-or-break duel with fate.

What Is the Future Outlook for Screenwriters?

Screenwriters are a pretty pessimistic group in general. Industry publications are full of laments over shrinking job prospects in Hollywood. In part this is because Hollywood studios take fewer risks on original scripts than they did in the past. They tend to stick with the tried-and-true box office successes and often turn to the same writers for new projects.

Television, however, has increasingly been attracting more talented screenwriters. The growing popularity of cable TV networks like HBO and Showtime has sparked renewed interest in writing for TV without the restrictions of traditional stations. As a result, more and more stations are making original shows that are winning praise for their creativity and originality. "TV is absolutely where the most dynamic, and honestly cinematic, writing is happening," says screenwriter John August in an interview with the online magazine *Creative Screenwriting*.

Video games are also a source of increasing employment for screenwriters. While few statistics are available on the specialized field, revenue for the industry in 2015 grew by more than 9 percent, indicating possible opportunities for video game screenwriters.

Find Out More

American Screenwriters Association (ASA)
website: http://americanscreenwriters.com

The ASA is an industry news and networking website intended to connect screenwriters to producers and others in the industry. The association also helps market scripts and performs other services for fees.

International Screenwriters' Association (ISA)
website: www.networkisa.org

The ISA is an online resource center for screenwriters. Its website includes links to continuing education, podcasts, teleconferences, agents, legal resources, and many other facets of screenwriting. Some content is free, and some is subscription based.

Script
website: www.scriptmag.com

Script is an online industry newsmagazine that offers articles on various aspects of script writing and trends in the industry. It also offers instructional links, interviews, webinars, and other educational resources, as well as reviews of books on script writing.

Scriptwriters Network
website: http://scriptwritersnetwork.com

The Scriptwriters Network is a nonprofit organization that cultivates contact between scriptwriters and others working on scripts of all sorts, including comic books, video games, TV, and film. Its website offers links to events and tips on the industry.

Writers Guild of America, West
7000 W. Third St.
Los Angeles, CA 90048
phone: (323) 951-4000
website: www.wga.org

The Writers Guild of America is a labor union for screenwriters and other types of writers. It evolved from the Screen Writers Guild, which was organized by Hollywood screenwriters in the 1930s. Today the organization is divided into branches covering the eastern and western United States. Its website contains useful links on both the writing of scripts and industry news. The group also organizes a video game writers' caucus.

Technical Writer

What Does a Technical Writer Do?

A technical writer's job exists between two worlds. On the one side is a technical profession, such as medicine, computer technology, or engineering. On the other is a reader who is generally unfamiliar with that profession but who needs to understand some basic information related to it.

Software engineers and high-tech manufacturers, for example, produce the mobile phones that are so much a part of life today. But just how do they explain the myriad functions of a smartphone to the user who buys it? This is where the technical writer comes in. Because many technical professionals speak in the highly specialized language of their professions, technical writers are hired to rework technical information into writing that is understandable to the layperson. In this regard, a technical writer performs much the same function as an interpreter, communicating between two groups that speak different languages. Because of the importance of communicating complex information from one

Keeping It Simple

"My job is to reduce a very detailed specification—in this case more than 122 pages—to a format that the user can understand. Users . . . want to reach their goal with as few clicks as possible. But I am told that this is the job of the usability team, not of the technical writer. I have to admit that he is basically right, but reply that my task is more than just describing the application. . . . It also involves ensuring, from the user's point of view, that the actual process for the user is as simple as possible."

Jan Rieker, "A Day in the Life of a Technical Writer," CLS Communication, April 30, 2015. www.cls-communication.com.

group to another, technical writers are also known as technical communicators.

That communication can come in the form of an instruction manual for a smartphone or DVD player, for example, but it comes in many other forms too. Technical writers often contribute to a company's website to convey information on technical products in language that is understandable to potential buyers. In this sense they support the advertising and marketing of products and services that a company would otherwise have trouble explaining to the general public.

If, for example, a company invents a complex new medical device, a technical writer might work on many aspects of the project's marketing. To help potential buyers understand the new product, a technical writer might post a clear description of the uses of the new device on the company's website, issue press releases to drum up interest from the media, and write up an advertising campaign to convey the essentials in clear, concise language. And of course, the writer will need to craft a detailed instruction manual to allow the end user to operate the new device.

Conveying complicated information to general readers might sound like a straightforward proposition. But once a technical writer understands all the complexities of a technical subject—through research, reading, and communicating with the technical team—the challenge is to convey this information to readers who might have unexpected questions. The technical writer, therefore, relies on imagination to conjure up all the potential questions that readers might have. "People often think a technical writer's job is as exciting as the proverbial bean counter in the field of accounting," writes Genise Caruso in the *Freelancer*, an online publication. "To say it's dull is laughable. . . . I never know what the next client may have up his or her sleeve, and trust me, it often challenges my skills."

Technical Background Not Essential

Most technical writers have attained at least a bachelor's degree. There are also an increasing number of academic programs designed for technical communications, which offer associate's, bachelor's, and master's degrees. These, however, are not strictly necessary to find a job as a technical writer. Above all the job is a writer's job, and therefore technical writers might have majored in English literature, journalism, or creative writing.

It is unquestionably valuable to have some training in science or math or the specific technical subject that you want to write about. But this too is not necessary to land a job as a technical writer. In fact, blog posts from technical writers list this as one of the biggest misconceptions about technical writing. "It's not such a bad thing if you're technically challenged," writes one technical writer on the blog *I'd Rather Be Writing*. "So are most of your users! You'll be on a level playing field and will probably write a help manual that actually speaks their language."

Skills and Personality

While a technical background is not strictly necessary to work as a technical writer, a highly detail-oriented nature is. You will need to have an insatiable desire to understand the myriad details of how things work and know how to conduct research to uncover this information. You will also need to be able to think logically, since you will be responsible for explaining, step-by-step, the ins and outs of complicated procedures and presenting them in a way that prevents confusion or ambiguity.

One major difference from other types of writing is that there will be little glory. Your name is unlikely to appear on anything you write, and your personality will remain in the background. Kurt Vonnegut, who majored in biochemistry and did some technical writing for General Electric before becoming a famous novelist, wrote that technical writers are "trained to reveal almost nothing about themselves in their writing. This makes them freaks in the world of writers, since almost all of the other ink-stained wretches in that world reveal a lot about themselves to the reader."

It will also be helpful if you like to work with people. You will need to work with the technical staff and quite possibly with other technical writers and a design team that helps craft the visual presentation of your writing, either online or in print. If you like interacting at work, love writing, and want to know how everything works, this might be a good writing job for you.

Lucrative in Comparison

Technical writers seem to take great pride in the fact that they can potentially earn more than other types of writing professions. The pay scale varies based on the employer, but because many technical writers are employed by highly profitable industries—high-tech manufacturers, software developers, or the pharmaceutical industry, for example—the pay can be quite good. In 2014, the median annual income was $69,030, according to the Bureau of Labor Statistics (BLS).

While some technical writers work full-time in a company or government agency, others work freelance, taking work on a project-by-project basis. These writers often charge an hourly rate, and in 2014 the average hourly rate was $33.19 per hour, according to the BLS. Peter Kent, the author of *Making Money in Technical Writing*, argues that technical writers can boost their salaries by charging a set fee for a project instead of an hourly rate and make more than $100,000 a year.

Employers Galore

One of the advantages to putting your writing skills to work as a technical writer is the range of employers. For computer companies and software companies, technical writers are an essential part of the marketing team. Pharmaceutical companies employ technical writers to help explain the complex health issues related to new drugs. Medical device manufacturers and large health care companies also make use of the same talent pool—technical writers who specialize in the medical field. Engineering companies also market their services with the help of technical writers. Nonprofit scientific research institutes and environmental policy groups also employ technical writers to explain their projects and findings to a wider audience. State and federal government agencies hire technical writers to explain technology and science and the public policy implications of new technologies.

A search on Indeed, a job-listing website, in January 2016 showed more than seventy-eight hundred openings for technical writers. The employers ranged from manufacturers to universities to the cable channel HBO.

Teamwork Required

Many writing jobs can be solitary by nature—just a writer pecking away on a computer. Not so with technical writing. It is a job that by nature requires constant communication. The technical writer must first understand the complex subject matter that will form the substance of the writing product—whether it is a user's manual, marketing materials for a company website, or an explanation of the steps of product development for use by company employees.

A typical day for a technical writer at an engineering or software firm might start with a meeting with a design and development team, followed by a test run of a specific product to see what issues might come up for a first-time user. This test phase might lead to more consultations and even revisions of the product or software to fix glitches that the technical writer has identified as not being user-friendly.

Once the technical writer feels confident enough that he or she understands the product or software, the writing phase can begin. But that might not yet mean the actual writing. The technical writer needs to know about the specific requirements of the materials he or she is producing—the length, the look, the audience, and the style. And this might first require a meeting with managers and the sales and marketing team to better understand what the writing is intended to accomplish.

If you have guessed that this consultation process takes up much of the day of a technical writer, you would be right. "Most tech writers spend about 10% of their time writing," notes technical writer Tom Johnson on the *I'd Rather Be Writing* blog.

Sluggish Job Advancement

Because technical writers tend to work with technical teams, it is not always easy to advance in the profession. There simply isn't

Writer as Translator

"Most of what I do is act as a buffer, a facilitator of information between whoever is writing the documentation, and the audience. Now, sometimes it's me writing the documentation, but sometimes it's someone else, say a software developer, who has intrinsic knowledge of the process he or she is trying to convey, but they are not a trained writer; that's more my thing. It's my job to get the information to the audience in the most clear and accessible way, so they can best understand."

Quoted in Dave Fruscalzo, "My Internship as a Technical Writer: What I Learnt," *Save the Semicolon* (blog), March 9, 2012. http://savethesemicolon.com.

much of a ladder to climb. That doesn't mean it can't be a well-paying, fulfilling job; it just means that technical writers often exist outside of an employer's hierarchy. A technical writer for a software company is unlikely, in other words, to become a software developer or the manager of software developers.

It is possible, however, to be promoted to a managerial level if a team of technical writers is employed by a company. And that team might also include sales and marketing personnel. Responsibilities might also be enlarged to include the development of strategies for marketing technical goods and services. These duties are generally carried out by a project manager, who often doesn't do a whole lot of writing.

The Future Outlook for Technical Writers

We live in a technologically obsessed world, and it is growing more complicated by the day. This is good news for technical writers, since the expansion of technical fields is creating jobs for technical writers at a rapid pace. In the decade from 2014 to 2024, the number of jobs is expected to grow by 10 percent, faster than other occupations, according to the BLS.

Find Out More

American Medical Writers Association (AMWA)
30 W. Gude Dr., Suite 525
Rockville, MD 20850-4347
phone: (240) 238-0940
website: www.amwa.org

The AMWA is a professional organization for technical writers specializing in medial issues. Its website offers educational resources, information about seminars and webinars, and career services, including surveys on salaries in the field.

Intercom

website: http://intercom.stc.org

A publication of the Society for Technical Communication, *Intercom* appears ten times a year and offers articles on professional development and samples of work by technical writers currently working in the field.

National Association of Science Writers (NASW)

PO Box 7905
Berkeley, CA 94707
phone: (510) 647-9500
website: www.nasw.org

The NASW was founded in 1934 by science journalists to promote more accurate scientific writing for the general public. Its website includes technical writing blogs on scientific subjects and links to jobs and career information. It also features free excerpts from *ScienceWriters* magazine, a publication of the association.

Society for Technical Communication (STC)

9401 Lee Hwy., Suite 300
Fairfax, VA 22031
phone: (703) 522-4114
website: www.stc.org

The STC is a professional association for technical writers. Its website offers free online educational tools, such as webinars and recorded seminars, as well as publications on industry news and job listings.

Lawyer

A Few Facts

Pay

In 2014 the median annual income for a lawyer was $114,970.

Professional Certification

Practicing law requires a law degree and the passage of the bar exam. In 2015 there were more than 1.3 million lawyers practicing in the United States.

Low Work Satisfaction

Among all professionals, lawyers are regularly the least satisfied with their professional life.

Lack of Diversity

Eighty-eight percent of US lawyers are white, making law one of the least diverse of all professions.

What Does a Lawyer Do?

You might not think of a lawyer as a writer, but when they are not talking, most of what lawyers do is write. "A huge hunk of a lawyer's day—when we aren't arguing cases or talking clients out of doing really dumb things . . . is taken up with writing pleadings, memos, and letters about what the law means and how it applies," explains attorney Jessica Mason in a 2015 article in *Bustle*, an online magazine.

The basic function of a lawyer is to assist clients in handling legal matters. Those clients include everyday people, corporations, and government agencies—really just about anyone who encounters a legal problem. The profession is divided into criminal law (think of a courtroom TV drama like *Law & Order*) and civil law. Criminal lawyers prosecute or defend legal cases that involve a possible violation of the law. The government initiates the proceedings by filing criminal charges. In civil law, private parties initiate lawsuits against other private parties.

Criminal lawyers tend to rely on writing less than lawyers engaged in civil law cases. And even in firms that deal mostly with civil cases, some types of lawyers will write more than others. For example, in a large corporate law firm, which will handle a variety of types of cases, some lawyers will advise on real estate or tax law, and others will draw up contracts for business mergers. They are performing legal services that require generally formulaic writing.

The scribblers of the profession tend to be engaged primarily in litigation—the work of shepherding a legal case through the court system. There are two sides to every case, but no matter which side a lawyer is on, there will be a flurry of written legal documents. The first is the complaint, which alleges legal wrongdoing and is filed with the court and delivered to the lawyers representing the person accused of wrongdoing. Next a response is drafted and filed with the court, and then lawyers draft motions trying to further their client's interest by including or excluding certain parts of the case. Both sides will write deposition questions and then question, or depose, relevant parties involved in the case. This is usually followed by more written motions.

At this point, some cases will be settled by the parties without going to trial, money exchanges hands, and the lawyer's job is done. If the case goes to trial, lawyers begin drafting another series of written documents—pretrial briefs, motions, opening statements, cross-examinations, and closing statements.

Law in the Real World

"Law school does not prepare you to practice law. Sure, it teaches you how to 'think like a lawyer,' but when you get your first job as an attorney, you will find that you're completely in the dark about a lot of things. Much of it is very specific to your practice area, and a lot of it is boring administrative stuff, like how to bill your hours."

Michael Helfand, "What Being a Lawyer Is Really Like," *Chicago's Real Law Blog*, April 11, 2012. www.chicagonow.com.

Because of the importance of writing, a common complaint from senior lawyers is that young lawyers can't write well. In part, this is because lawyers, above all, must write compellingly—they must convince other people to agree with their written arguments. Studies have shown that the most effective written arguments often contain a compelling story. "A growing body of literature indicates that most people, including judges, make decisions more readily on the basis of stories that they can relate to their own experiences that they do through argument, statistics, or logic," writes Mark K. Osbeck in the *Drexel Law Review*.

Law School a Must

To become a lawyer you must attain certain qualifications. These start with a college degree. Some of the more common majors for lawyers are economics, history, political science, and international relations, but you could study just about anything so long as your grades are good enough to get into a law school. Students take the Law School Admission Test before applying to law school. This standardized test measures reading comprehension skills, critical thinking, and logic—and scores provide a numerical measurement for eligibility to a law school.

The next step is law school, usually a three-year program that trains lawyers in basic legal principles and the practice of both oral and written argument. Between the second and third years of law school, law students generally apply for competitive summer associate programs at law firms. The summer programs introduce students to the profession in a more practical sense and provide personal connections to working lawyers. A summer program will often lead to a job offer at the same law firm. Students at the top of their class are also generally invited to write for a law school's law review, or student legal publication, which gives them additional writing experience and a certain prestige among the student body.

The final step before officially becoming a lawyer is the passage of the bar exam, a test administered by the bar association, a government licensing body for lawyers, in the state in which you want to practice law.

Skills and Personality

Because of the wide range of jobs in the legal profession, many different personality types can be found within a law firm. Contract lawyers, for example, tend to be a more social bunch since they focus on facilitating deals between clients. Tax law, on the other hand, often appeals to people who like math and are highly detail oriented. Litigation, the most writing-intensive part of the profession, tends to attract people who like to argue. If you grew up debating with your friends, questioning everything, and taking pleasure in winning an argument, practicing litigation might be a good fit for your personality.

Big Bucks

A frequent complaint among young lawyers is the debt they accumulate during law school. Law school is expensive, and few scholarships are offered. In part this is because law schools know that lawyers will generally be well paid once they find employment.

In 2014 the median income for a lawyer was $114,970 per year, a considerably higher salary than most professions that require a love of writing.

The pay scale is, in fact, one of the main draws of the profession, and raises and bonuses are generally given on an annual basis. A first-year corporate lawyer, for example, can earn as much as $105,000 at a small firm and as much as $160,000 at a large firm. Partners, who are technically owners of a law firm, can make considerably more than the median average and sometimes have annual salaries that reach into the millions.

Who's Hiring?

Lawyers generally work for a few different types of employers. Law firms and the government are probably the most obvious. But lawyers also work on staff at all kinds of private companies to advise employers on legal issues, and lawyers who do this type of work are known as in-house counsel. Lawyers are also hired by public interest groups, civic associations, hospitals, and many other groups that frequently require legal advice.

In January 2016 a search of LawCrossing, a popular job-search website for the legal profession, listed 163,221 jobs, of which more than 48,000 were added in the previous week. The majority of the listings were for corporate lawyers who work at law firms, but there were also a significant number of openings for in-house lawyers (12,254), government lawyers (1,731), and public interest lawyers (928). Corporate jobs, in general, however, are usually obtained not through Internet searches but through the summer programs offered by law firms as a recruiting mechanism.

Be Ready for Long Hours

Work life for lawyers varies considerably, based partly on the type of law they practice. Of course, there are some constants—you'll most likely be in an office and at the beck and call of clients and more senior lawyers. But if you work in-house in a company's legal department (say for a newspaper or a large tech company like Yahoo! or Google), you will at least have more predictable hours—and if you are lucky, a nine-to-five schedule. The same is also true of government lawyers and many who work in public interest law (for environmental groups, child welfare agencies, and other social welfare and advocacy groups).

For lawyers who try cases in a litigation department at a large corporate law firm, the story is altogether different. Lawyers who are just starting their careers can be saddled with fifty to sixty-five hours of work a week. The working hours get shorter as one gains seniority, but the workload is a common complaint among young litigators.

This heavy workload can take its toll. A 2013 survey conducted by CareerBliss, a company that tracks workplace satisfaction, found that among the many professions surveyed, associate lawyers (lawyers who have not yet made partner) reported that they were the least happy with their workplace environment.

The long hours are particularly hard on women who would like to start a family, since there is little time for anything aside from work in the early years. "The legal environment in which women practice is one that has been designed in a male model," explained Deborah Epstein Henry, a former lawyer, in an article on the *Daily Beast* news website. "It's a model that works best when you have somebody at home taking care of all the details of your life."

As a result, women tend to leave the profession at much higher rates than men, and fewer of them make it to partner. While women account for about 40 percent of law school graduates, only 17 percent were equity partners at major law firms, according to a 2013 survey by the National Association of Women Lawyers.

Becoming a Partner

Despite the high levels of dissatisfaction among young lawyers, career advancement at a law firm is an annual ritual. In fact,

lawyers refer to new hires as first-year associates, then second-year associates, and so on. With each passing year, a raise is common—and quite often a bonus—and the number of hours in the office starts to decline. By the seventh or eighth year (although this number varies at different law firms), an associate will be considered for promotion to partner. Those who make partner will enter the senior ranks of the firm, and those who don't will usually find their way to another law firm or another profession. Becoming a partner is a major milestone in the career of a corporate lawyer.

What Is the Future Outlook for Lawyers?

Inside the legal profession, there has been a great deal of hand-wringing over future job prospects for lawyers. Some believe that new technologies will take over some of the daily tasks of law associates (such as research), and therefore the profession will shrink as a whole. Others believe that a trend toward clients rejecting high legal fees will cause a slowdown in hiring. Despite

Making Partner

"You now occupy a new professional status, and the nature of making partner is such that no matter how badly you screw up the rest of your life, you have accomplished something very rare. It is a life milestone, on par with getting married or winning the lottery in terms of its immediate alteration of your identity."

Anonymous partner at a New York law firm, quoted in David Lat, "Is Being a Partner the Worst Job in Biglaw?," Above the Law, June 22, 2013. http://abovethelaw.com.

these trends, jobs for lawyers are expected to grow by 6 percent between 2014 and 2024, according to the Bureau of Labor Statistics.

No matter what the job growth is, jobs for lawyers will remain highly competitive. Law schools routinely train more lawyers than the profession can employ. In 2014 only 66.3 percent of law school graduates were employed in jobs that required passage of the bar exam, according to a survey conducted by the National Association for Law Placement.

Find Out More

ABA for Law Students
website: http://abaforlawstudents.com

This website hosted by the American Bar Association offers a wide range of information on law school and how to enter the legal profession, including study aides, information on upcoming conferences, and resource guides to finding jobs in specific fields of the legal profession.

Above the Law
website: http://abovethelaw.com

Above the Law provides an insiders' look at the legal profession with articles on all aspects of the legal profession. It features information on law firms big and small, in-house legal jobs, law schools, and professional news. It also features a career center.

American Bar Association (ABA)
Chicago Headquarters
321 North Clark St.
Chicago, IL 60654
phone: (312) 988-5000
website: www.americanbar.org

The ABA is a nationwide professional association for lawyers and law students, with chapters scattered across the United States. It works to formulate academic standards for law schools and ethical standards and continuing education programs for practicing attorneys. The ABA website provides information on changes in the profession and on changing educational trends in the field.

National Association for Law Placement (NALP)
1220 Nineteenth St. NW, Suite 401
Washington, DC 20036
phone: (202) 835-1001
website: www.nalp.org

The NALP is an association of legal professionals who advise law students and map out some of the profession's employment trends. Its website includes information on conferences, recruitment and other career services, and detailed research on trends in legal employment.

Vault
website: www.vault.com/company-rankings/law

Vault is a corporate rankings website that gives detailed information on corporate culture, salaries, and other information based on lawyers' feedback. It is commonly used by lawyers and law students who are looking for a law firm that best suits particular skills and personality types.

INTERVIEW WITH A LAWYER

Robert Turner is the senior legal director for commercial litigation at Yahoo!, where he has worked for three-plus years after nearly a decade in private practice. He spoke with the author about his career.

Q: Why did you become a lawyer?

A: Although I am a third generation lawyer, I spent many years trying to find something other than the law to pursue as my career. Ultimately, however, I realized that everything that interested me most could trace directly back to the law. I loved reading and writing and arguing. But while I had thought about becoming an academic, ultimately I wanted to effect change. Becoming a lawyer was the best way to combine all of those interests with my desire to win.

Q: Can you describe your typical workday?

A: There's nothing typical about any of my workdays, though there is a common theme—effective communication. My role at Yahoo requires me to manage lawsuits filed against the company around the world, which involves finding, retaining, and directing external lawyers to represent Yahoo in court, coordinating Yahoo's internal response and involvement in any given lawsuit, and ultimately putting our management in the best position to make strategic decisions. In any given day, however, this process could involve responding to a new lawsuit, meeting with employees to prepare them for deposition or trial, reading and editing legal briefs, pleadings, and other documents, or providing guidance and strategy for lawsuits and other issues faced by the company.

Key to this job, and my daily activity, however, is effective communication. Throughout my day I am in contact with other Yahoo lawyers, businesspeople both at Yahoo and elsewhere, opposing counsel, and government representatives. These conversations happen over e-mail, or in letters, over the phone, in person, or via video conference. The one thing I can count on when I show up for work in the morning is that, whether it's scheduled or not, I'll be in communication all day. Because of this, the greatest skill one can have in my job is the ability to think on one's feet and communicate clearly, efficiently, and effectively.

Q: What do you like most and least about your job?

A: Every day is a new challenge. I'm constantly getting a chance to expand my knowledge, learn new skills, and meet new people. I also really love speaking with and working with others. Working as an in-house lawyer, or really as any sort of lawyer, is an exercise in collaboration.

The only negative of being a lawyer is that while the law does change, it tends to do so slowly. Only in rare cases do litigators force change; rather, our work is part of the larger process by which Congress or regulatory agencies effect broad societal and governmental change.

Q: What personal qualities do you find most valuable for this type of work?

A: Litigating is not for the faint of heart. You need to be steady in your convictions even in the face of long odds. You need to be persistent, patient, and at times aggressive. And above all, you need to be an effective communicator, within whatever constraints (whether in time or space) you're given.

Q: What advice do you have for students who might be interested in this career?

A: It's helpful to always be curious. One of the hallmarks of working as a litigator is that every case is an opportunity to learn something new, whether an industry, product, or area of law. It's also important to begin thinking about ways to develop your own voice. Not all litigators need to be great orators, but we all need to be great communicators of ideas. If your interest is in writing, spend time crafting your own written voice. If you love speaking and are quick on your feet, give yourself as many opportunities as you can to find out what works and what doesn't work, whether through debate, school government, etc.

Q: How important is writing to your career, and what makes for good legal writing?

A: Although the popular image of a litigator is of a solitary lawyer persuading a jury through oral argument, the fact of litigation is that 90 percent of the work is done in writing. You can be a litigator without being a tremendous orator, but you cannot be a litigator without being a good writer. Every case is a story, and our job is to tell that story in the most effective way possible. The task of the litigator is to digest every possible aspect of a case and distill that to the most important, and ultimately persuasive, story.

Q: What was your favorite subject in school?

A: I was always an avid reader and gravitated toward English classes and history. The need for a solid background in writing and composition is clear, but I have absorbed so much from literature that informs my own personal voice and style. As for history, the law is steeped in history, and history is steeped in lawyers.

Q: Did you ever think about doing something else?

A: Before I decided to pursue being a lawyer, I was convinced that I would become a teacher or professor. Teachers had done so much to shape my life that I wanted to be able to have a similar impact. Ultimately, the skill set is pretty analogous; although I do still think about teaching, I get to use the law and my storytelling skills to teach judges, juries, and the public at large about my case and why I should win.

OTHER CAREERS IF YOU LIKE WRITING

Acquisitions Editor
Arts Reviewer
Banking Analyst
Book Author
Book Editor
Book Reviewer
Catalogue Copywriter
Children's Book Author
Columnist
Comic Book Author
Copy Editor
Editorial Assistant in a
   Publishing House
English Teacher
Executive Assistant
Food Writer
Foreign Service Officer
Ghost Writer
Government Communications
   Officer

Greeting Card Writer
Intelligence Analyst
Investor Relations
Librarian
Literary Agent
Literature Professor
Novelist
Playwright
Policy Analyst
Proofreader
Reading Tutor
Researcher
Résumé and Cover Letter
   Writer
Songwriter
Speechwriter
Translator
Travel Writer
Writing Coach
Writing Professor

Editor's note: The online *Occupational Outlook Handbook* of the US Department of Labor's Bureau of Labor Statistics is an excellent source of information on jobs in hundreds of career fields, including many of those listed here. The *Occupational Outlook Handbook* may be accessed online at www.bls.gov/ooh.

INDEX

28`45